DANIEL IN THE LION'S DEN

Bible Bedtime Story

BLUME POTTER

INTRODUCTION

As you tuck your little ones into bed each night, there's a special opportunity to fill their dreams with stories that not only entertain but also inspire. Daniel in the Lion's Den is more than just a tale from the Bible; it's a story of unwavering faith, bravery, and the power of standing up for what is right, even in the face of the fiercest challenges.

This book is crafted with love and care, designed to captivate the hearts and minds of children aged 3 to 8. Through the story of Daniel, your child or grandchild will embark on a journey where they will learn about the importance of trusting in God, being courageous, and the incredible miracles that can happen when one remains faithful.

Each chapter is filled with gentle, engaging prose that will make bedtime not just a routine, but a cherished moment of bonding and reflection. As Daniel faces the lions, your little ones will learn that true strength comes from within, and that with faith, anything is possible.

Let this book be a treasured part of your child's or grandchild's bedtime routine—a story that will leave them feeling comforted, inspired, and ready to face the world with the same courage and faith as Daniel.

CHAPTER 1:
DANIEL'S FAITHFULNESS

In the heart of a vast and prosperous kingdom, there lived a man named Daniel. Daniel was known far and wide for his wisdom, kindness, and unwavering faith in God. He wasn't born into royalty, nor did he come from a wealthy family, but his character and devotion set him apart. People from all walks of life admired Daniel, for he was not only a wise counselor to the king but also a man of great humility and integrity.

Daniel had served many kings throughout his life, always with the same dedication and honesty. He had a special way of solving problems that no one else could. When disputes arose in the kingdom, Daniel's advice was always fair and just. His wisdom seemed to come from a higher place, and everyone who met him could see that Daniel was a man close to God.

Every day, without fail, Daniel would rise early in the morning, long before the sun peeked over the hills. He would open the windows of his room, face toward Jerusalem, and pray to God. Daniel's prayers were filled with gratitude, asking for guidance and strength to continue serving the king and his people with honor. His prayers were so sincere that anyone who heard them would feel a sense of peace and hope.

The people of the kingdom loved Daniel. They knew that his wisdom came from his deep faith, and they respected him for it. Even the king, who had many advisors, valued

Daniel's counsel above all others. The king often said, "Daniel is like a beacon of light in this kingdom. His wisdom guides us, and his faith inspires us."

But not everyone shared the king's admiration for Daniel. There were a few high-ranking officials in the court who were envious of the favor Daniel had with the king. They couldn't understand why a man who was not of noble birth could be so loved and respected. These officials were proud and ambitious, and they saw Daniel as an obstacle to their own rise to power.

"Why should Daniel, a foreigner, be so close to the king?" one of the officials would mutter under his breath.

"His influence over the king is too great," another would agree. "If we don't do something, he will always stand in our way."

These officials would watch Daniel from a distance, their eyes narrowed with envy. They saw how Daniel's wisdom and kindness won the hearts of the people, and it made them furious. They would whisper among themselves, plotting and scheming, trying to find a way to bring Daniel down.

But Daniel, in his wisdom, was unaware of their jealousy. He continued to serve the king faithfully, praying to God three times a day, just as he had always done. He knew that his strength and wisdom came from God, and nothing could shake his faith.

As the days passed, the officials' jealousy grew stronger. They knew that they could not accuse Daniel of anything dishonest, for he was a man of integrity. But they were determined to find a way to rid themselves of him. They began to watch Daniel more closely, hoping to find some fault, some way to turn the king against him.

Little did they know, their scheming would soon set in motion a series of events that would test Daniel's faith like never before. But Daniel, with his unwavering trust in God, was ready for whatever challenges lay ahead. His faithfulness would be his strength, and through it, he would show the entire kingdom the power of standing firm in one's beliefs, no matter the cost.

CHAPTER 2:
THE KING'S DECREE

Word spread quickly throughout the kingdom that a new law was being discussed in the royal court. The officials who envied Daniel had finally devised a plan to trap him. They approached the king with their proposal, their voices dripping with false flattery.

"O mighty king," they began, bowing low before the throne, "you are the greatest ruler this kingdom has ever known. It is only right that your subjects honor you above all others. We suggest a new decree: for the next thirty days, no one in the kingdom may pray to any god or man except you, O king. Anyone who disobeys this law should be thrown into the lion's den."

The king, pleased with the idea of being honored in such a way, agreed. He didn't realize that this decree was a trap set for his most trusted advisor, Daniel. Without thinking of the consequences, the king sealed the law with his royal signet, making it unchangeable.

When Daniel heard about the new law, his heart remained steadfast. He knew that his loyalty belonged to God above all else. He would not let fear of the lions stop him from praying. Just as he always had, Daniel went to his room, opened his windows, and knelt down to pray, facing Jerusalem. His prayers were filled with the same love and devotion he had always shown, trusting that God would watch over him.

The jealous officials had been waiting for this moment. They crept to Daniel's house and, peeking through the windows, saw him praying. A wicked smile spread across their faces. They had caught Daniel breaking the king's decree, and now they had the evidence they needed.

The officials hurried back to the palace and reported what they had seen to the king. "Your Majesty," they said, trying to hide their glee, "we have found someone who has disobeyed your decree. It is Daniel, your most trusted advisor. He continues to pray to his God, despite the law you have set."

The king's heart sank. He realized that he had been tricked into signing a decree that would harm the very man he respected most. The king admired Daniel's faithfulness and didn't want to punish him. But the law was unchangeable, even by the king himself.

With a heavy heart, the king ordered Daniel to be arrested. The guards, though reluctant, followed the king's command and led Daniel away. The king watched, torn between his duty to uphold the law and his deep fondness for Daniel.

As Daniel was brought before the king, there was no fear in his eyes. His faith in God remained unshaken, and he knew that whatever happened, he had done what was right. The king, struggling with guilt, whispered to Daniel, "May your God, whom you serve so faithfully, deliver you."

Daniel was sentenced to be thrown into the lion's den, a place from which no one had ever returned. The officials smirked, thinking they had finally rid themselves of Daniel. But they underestimated the power of Daniel's faith and the God he served. As the night fell, and the entrance to the lion's den was sealed, Daniel prayed once more, trusting in God to protect him from the danger that lay ahead.

CHAPTER 3:
IN THE LION'S DEN

As the sun began to set, the sky turned shades of orange and pink, casting long shadows over the kingdom. Daniel stood calmly surrounded by guards as they led him toward the dreaded lion's den. The roar of the hungry lions echoed through the air, sending chills down the spines of everyone nearby. But Daniel's face remained peaceful, his eyes filled with unwavering trust in God.

At the entrance of the den, the guards hesitated for a moment, uneasy about what they were ordered to do. The king arrived, his face full of sorrow and regret. He looked at Daniel and said softly, "May your God, whom you serve so faithfully, rescue you." Daniel smiled kindly at the king, nodding in gratitude before he was lowered into the dark pit below.

Inside the den, the ground was cold and the air was thick with the smell of the wild beasts. The lions circled around Daniel, their golden eyes gleaming and their massive paws padding silently on the stone floor. They were strong and hungry, their mouths opening wide to reveal sharp, gleaming teeth. But Daniel did not tremble or cry out. Instead, he closed his eyes, knelt down, and began to pray, speaking softly to God and trusting in His protection.

Above, the guards rolled a heavy stone over the entrance of the den, sealing Daniel inside with the fierce lions. The night grew dark, and silence fell over the kingdom. While others slept, Daniel continued his prayers, his heart filled with faith. Suddenly, a bright light filled the den, and an angel appeared beside Daniel, radiating warmth and peace. The angel gently touched each lion, and immediately, their mouths closed, and their fierce growls turned into soft purrs.

The lions lay down around Daniel, calm and harmless, as if they were gentle kittens. One even rested its great head near Daniel's feet, closing its eyes in sleep. Daniel smiled, feeling safe and comforted by God's miraculous protection. Throughout the night, he rested peacefully among the lions, knowing that God had heard his prayers and sent His angel to keep him safe.

As dawn approached, the first light of morning crept into the sky, promising a new day and revealing the wonders that faith and trust in God could bring.

CHAPTER 4:
A MIRACLE IN THE MORNING

As the first light of dawn began to spread across the kingdom, the king tossed and turned in his bed, unable to sleep. His thoughts were consumed by worry for Daniel, the trusted advisor he had sentenced to the lion's den. At the first sign of morning, the king leaped from his bed and hurried to the den, his heart pounding with fear and hope.

When the king arrived at the den, he ordered the stone to be rolled away. The guards quickly obeyed, and as the heavy stone was moved aside, the king leaned forward, his voice trembling as he called out, "Daniel, servant of the living God, has your God, whom you serve so faithfully, been able to rescue you from the lions?"

For a moment, there was silence. The king held his breath, dreading what he might hear. But then, from deep within the den, a calm and steady voice responded, "O king, live forever! My God sent His angel, and He shut the mouths of the lions. They have not hurt me because I was found innocent in His sight. Nor have I ever done any wrong before you, O king."

The king's face lit up with joy and relief. "Lift Daniel out of the den immediately!" he commanded, his voice filled with excitement. The guards quickly lowered a rope, and with steady hands, they pulled Daniel up from the pit. As Daniel emerged from the darkness, the king rushed forward, embracing him with gratitude and awe.

There wasn't a scratch on Daniel; he was completely unharmed. The king marveled at the miracle that had taken place. "Truly, your God is the living God," the king declared, "and He has rescued you from the power of the lions."

The entire kingdom soon learned of the miraculous event, and the king's admiration for Daniel grew even stronger. He knew that Daniel's God was real and powerful, and he rejoiced that Daniel had been saved. The king's joy was shared by the people, who celebrated the miracle and praised Daniel's unwavering faith.

As the sun rose higher in the sky, shining brightly over the kingdom, Daniel looked up with a grateful heart. He knew that God's protection and faithfulness had saved him, and he was more determined than ever to continue serving with wisdom and faith. The miracle in the morning was a testament to the power of standing firm in one's beliefs, and it became a story that would be told and retold for generations to come.

CHAPTER 5:
A NEW LAW OF FAITH

The news of Daniel's miraculous escape from the lion's den spread like wildfire throughout the kingdom. People gathered in the streets, talking in hushed voices about the man who had been saved by his God. The king, deeply moved by what had happened, knew that this miracle was not just a sign of Daniel's faith, but of the true power of Daniel's God.

The king summoned all his officials and the people of the kingdom to the palace courtyard. With a voice full of authority and reverence, he addressed the crowd. "Let it be known throughout the land," the king proclaimed, "that Daniel's God is the living God, who endures forever. His kingdom will never be destroyed, and His dominion will never end. He rescues and saves; He performs signs and wonders in the heavens and on the earth. He has saved Daniel from the power of the lions."

The king's words echoed through the courtyard, and the people listened with rapt attention. "Therefore," the king continued, "I issue a new decree: that in every part of my kingdom, people must respect and worship the God of Daniel. For He alone is worthy of our praise and devotion."

The crowd murmured in agreement, their hearts filled with awe at the king's declaration. The jealous officials who had plotted against Daniel hung their heads in shame, knowing that their plan had backfired. Instead of bringing Daniel down, they had only strengthened his standing in the kingdom.

From that day forward, the people of the kingdom honored Daniel's God, and Daniel himself was held in even higher regard than before. The king bestowed upon him great honors, and Daniel continued to serve faithfully, always staying true to his faith in God. His wisdom guided the kingdom, and his story became a shining example of the power of faith and the importance of standing up for what is right.

As the years passed, the tale of Daniel and the lion's den was told in every corner of the kingdom. Children grew up hearing about the man who trusted in God and was saved from the jaws of lions. Daniel's legacy lived on, a testament to the power of faith and the unwavering protection of a loving God.

And so, Daniel's days were filled with peace and joy, knowing that his faith had not only saved his life but had also brought the entire kingdom closer to the God he served so faithfully.